Willem M. Roggeman

# WHAT ONLY PAINTERS SEE
## Selected Poems

*translated from Dutch
and edited by
Philippe Ernewein*

BAMBOO
DART
PRESS

LOS ANGELES † NEW YORK † LONDON † MELBOURNE

*What only painters see* by Willem M. Roggeman,
translated by Philippe Ernewein

978-1-947240-65-0        Paperback
978-1-947240-66-7        eBook

First Printing 2023


Front cover painting by Fred Bervoets: "Self Portrait," colored
etching on paper, 100 x 70 cm, 2012

Interior drawing by Marc Mendelson: No title, India ink on paper,
22 x 30cm, 1968

Back cover painting by Maurice Wyckaert: Mixed border, oil on
canvas, 50 x 70 cm, 1993

Layout and design by Mark Givens

For information:

Bamboo Dart Press

chapbooks@bamboodartpress.com


Supported by a grant from

Bamboo Dart Press 029

www.pelekinesis.com

www.bamboodartpress.com

SHRiMPER

www.shrimperrecords.com

# A PAINTER WITH WORDS

Few writers have such an intense and lifelong relationship with the world of fine arts as the Flemish poet Willem M. Roggeman. This collection captures the poetic narrative and insight of that relationship. As the Flemish poet, artist, and critic Paul De Vree so accurately described, Willem M. Roggeman is "a painter with words."

Since he was 18 years old, he regularly visited art galleries in his native city Brussels. Sharing this relationship with the world in the form of publishing poems started at age twenty-one when he won an important poetry prize awarded by the avant-garde group "De Nevelvlek" (The Nebula) in Antwerp, Belgium. They published his first poems in their literary magazine *Het Cahier* (The Exercise Book).

A month later he read his poems for the first time to an audience at the avant-garde centre Taptoe in Brussels. There he made the acquaintance of the renowned Danish painter Asger Jorn, who later founded the artistic group COBRA, an acronym for Copenhagen, Brussels, and Amsterdam, the home cities of the collective's founders.

In Taptoe he also met the Chinese painter Walasse Ting, whose art was on exhibit. Ting later emigrated to the United States and received global recognition. Roggeman became close friends with the Belgian painters Maurice Wyckaert and Serge Vandercam, both of whom are recognized in this collection.

After his national service in the Belgian Army, Roggeman started working for the popular Flemish newspaper *Het Laatste Nieuws* in Brussels. He wrote thousands of columns reviewing and critiquing literature and art exhibitions.

After twenty years as a journalist, he became assistant director of the Flemish Cultural Centre de Brakke Grond in Amsterdam, where he was the curator of the exhibitions of Flemish painters and sculptors. As an art critic, he wrote for several art magazines including *Kunstbeeld* in Amsterdam and *Kunst en Cultuur*, the magazine published by the Palace of Fine Arts in Brussels.

Among his friends are the Dutch painters Bram Bogart and Lucebert, and the Flemish painters Pol Mara, Roger Raveel, Marc Mendelson, Jan Burssens, Jan Cox (Professor at the Art Academy in Boston), Godfried Vervisch and Fred Bervoets.

In 2002, Roggeman traveled with the artist Fred Bervoets (b. 1942) to Moscow, where the painter had an exhibition at the university and the poet had a presentation of a book with his poems in Russian translation.

Willem M. Roggeman also met many American poets. He introduced Robert Lowell and Gregory Corso at the international poetry festival in Rotterdam, Netherlands where he also read his translations of the poems they were reading. He interviewed Denise Levertov for Flemish television and met Allen Ginsberg and Robert Creely at different poetry festivals where he was also a featured poet. He traveled twice through the United States in the 1960s. During his journey in 1966, he visited Lawrence Ferlinghetti in his City Lights Bookstore in San Francisco. At a Congress of PEN International in New York, he spoke with Arthur Miller and Saul Bellow.

It is clear that the poetry of Willem M. Roggeman is more influenced by the paintings he has sought out and admired, than by the writings of other poets. This is illuminated not only by the subject matter of several of his poems but also by his particular way of writing.

In contrast with the common habits of poets who stress the musical aspect and the rhythm of their verses, Roggeman strives for visual poetry with images that provoke the imagination of the reader.

When I met him in Brussels, Belgium for an interview, Willem M. Roggeman told me that during his service in the Belgian Army, he would pack "a suitcase full of books to read" whenever afforded a break from the duty of his assigned post. This collection is like that suitcase, bound neatly in a single volume, full of poems that will open a keen lens on art and ways of seeing and understanding the world of the artist. It is brought to us by the poet whose page is his canvas and his pen the brush.

**Philippe Ernewein**
Denver, Colorado, USA

# CONTENTS

# ARS POETICA

This book falls with a bang and stays open
and the whole world rolls out of it quite astonished.
Only now, the language plunges into reality.
The reader groans under its weight.

There will always be more people than verses,
even if one adds the dead languages and dialects,
for writing is setting traps for words,
which falter when faced with the deaf ears of the age.

Only by keeping quiet can one evoke amazement.
But the writer keeps hunting for questions
even as far as Alexandria into another era,
driving them further into a pious dumb domain.

In the whimsical dark shapes of the clouds
he deciphers the delirious woman of Delphi.
He gives her a voice, hardly noticing her.
Her words sing within him like a poem.

# RAW MATERIAL FOR A POEM

Real and rowdy frogs suddenly jump up
in Marianne Moore's imaginary garden.

She takes off her reading glasses and looks myopically
out of an existing window at fictitious shrubs.

Then she writes very simple words down,
a rough draft of modest material,

in a surprising and inexplicable manner
almost corresponding to reality.

She puts on her hat and disappears absentmindedly
into the white spaces between the lines of her poem.

# COLUMBUS IN NEW YORK

When Columbus discovered America
he couldn't believe his eyes.
He'd come with his shipmates
in search of a guru
and really set his sights on India.
But as his ship the Santa Maria
was on the point of sinking he was picked up
by the harbor police and sailed
past the Statue of Liberty and a bit later
was craning up among the skyscrapers.
I'll have to tell my queen about this, he thought.
Who'd have expected skyscrapers in India?
Next morning his picture was splashed across
the front page of the New York Herald Tribune
and shares in Indian hemp
rocketed in Wall Street.
In a sleazy dive in the Bowery
Columbus gave himself a fix
and in a whirling of colors
imagined himself commander
of a fifteenth century Spanish caravel.

# LOCKDOWN

Some can't take it anymore.
Some paint a mirror on the wall
with the face of a woman in it.
Some listen to a tape
with the voice of a woman
whose whispering can hardly be heard.
Some feed their imagination
with recollections of adventures
they never experienced.
Some see in the creases
of the blanket on the bed
the shape of a sleeping woman.
Some feel asleep
with one hand in the hand of the night.
Some whisper I love you
and listen to the stove's answer.
Some can't agree with themselves.
Some know the precise personal description
of a woman they never knew.
Some point to the place
where alcohol gave birth to beauty.
Some sit motionless in a room

and travel with dizzying speed
through the country that begins behind the mirror.
Some are afraid of the sunrise.
Some answer the questions
that no-one ever asked them
Due to lack of interest.
Some see in the wallpaper
how life passes by.
Some can't even talk to themselves.
Some don't realize that yesterday has never begun.
Some sink like stones into time.
Some feel their bood stop running.
No one is alone in his loneliness.

# WHAT ONLY PAINTERS SEE

These are the first signs:
A startled moon between the trees.
Animals starting to stutter.
Flowers stirring from a nightmare.

Humans terrified of the future
scurry back into the trees.
The night gapes at the darkness.
Everything that ever happened drops out of time.

Silence steals its way upwards.
Old men degenerate into light.
He who keeps vigil, preserves
the melancholy trellis of his dreams for nought.

Sleep forsakes our eyes unseen.
Our fears scream loud and louder.
The spring tries on its new attire.
The sun slithers beyond the sea.

Evening enters every home
unrecognized by daylight.
Another day, another flash.
Look lightning, someone repeats after us.

# Twenty Years After Pol Mara

The idealistic realism is being replaced,
ending up in fragments, where Pol Mara
introduces the inhabitants of his dreams.

Was this previously ever highlighted?
The world, unfortunately, does not have the talent
to always look so seductive.

Fiction was built upon with the assistance
of a movie actress, a picture from a television screen,
or photos from illustrated magazines.

Every painting, every watercolor invites you
inside with the intimate company
that is far too beautiful to be a lie.

In this imperial summer month,
all the women he ever featured in his art,
unleash their defenseless smiles on you.

After traveling through America, Japan, and Kathmandu,
where he spoke with people of various points of view,
he looked like a stranger to his neighbors.

A figurative idea: in the car on the way
to Gordes in the Vaucluse, to that low
white house with a swimming pool on top of a mountain,

with the valley in the distance, on the other side,
the ruins of the castle where the Marquis
de Sade wrote his fantasies of Justine.

And there are two novels in the backseat,
"Jean le Blue" and "Colline" by Jean Giono,
books with the purple scent of Provence.

A hazy mist in the early morning
bears the signature of summer.
The hills keep silent about their thistles.
The meadows are astonished to see glass horses
trot silently and invisibly toward the night.
And a praying mantis begs loudly for rain.

With photographic precision Mara paints
here his poetic vision of city life:
a beautiful woman in her apartment in her underwear.

He resembled Woody Allen, the actor,
so convincingly that in America
he was not allowed to pay his hotel bill.

Everything taken out of life
and assembled in the studio in Antwerp,
translated into new flawless images.

And the year 1998 came into view,
a year that would only last till February.

Until then the adventure seemed endless.

# A Ghost Wrapped in Paint
## *for Serge Vandercam*

Lost in time like a long forgotten name
in a language so often changed since its origin
with always the futile waiting for the surprise
in a year that started prematurely and speechless.

Those who declared it still don't know
that at this moment everything becomes historical truth.
But the alienation closed its hands around it
once it turned out that lust and love form an alliteration.

The nights grow unrecognizable during sleep
with their underestimated signs of the zodiac still speaking
with rhymes in an antiquated manner as an introduction
or a comparison with a time when the words
become no longer visible and scarcer to everyone.

A painter stands with mythological gestures
and shouting in the midst of his blissful garden
and in amazement sees a wooden bird fly up.

# THE PHENOMENOLOGY OF PERCEPTION

Something completely transparent,
to look carefully at this.
To know it is there
and yet not see it.
Eyes feel deceived.
About their working order
there is suddenly a doubt.
They hesitate between what is real
and what still needs to be believed.
This is a strange sensation.
To look through something
while feeling there is nothing there.

# MILAN LATE IN THE MORNING

Because every morning the city draws a different shape.
And every time she also gracefully rewrites her family name.
The Duomo then juggles its thousands of statuettes.

The clouds occasionally look like sheepskin.
An opened window at the residence of Manzoni
offers a distant view all the way back in time.

In the Santa Maria delle Grazie church
five centuries are attached to one wall
like faded colors of a fresco.

Thirteen people sit at a table
and eat together for their last meal.
In one alcove Leonardo plays the accordion.

Outside a passerby starts to rust.
A long unemployed verb stands by.
A crumpled up ball of newspaper
rolls over the stones of the street after a car.

At the edge of the big round plaza
that is named Piazza Meda but is actually
a bulge of the Corso Matteotti
where the cars race at breakneck speed

stands the sculpture of Arnaldo Pomodoro,
an enormous bronze disc standing upright
on its one-and-a-half-meter wide side.
Polished, it shines dazzled in the sun.

On the round surface of this sculpture
dozens of vertical notches are etched
as double rays in all directions
an inspired, unreadable text in relief,
poetry recorded in an unearthly language.

Nearby the Scala searches for perfection,
while aria's from Guiseppe Verdi sing
between lost gestures of a swan
someone praises the icons of unification.

Leisurely walking on the greatly expanded avenue
Umberto Eco shifts all the layers of meaning
in his novel "The Name of the Rose".
The obsessive cadence of the Metro's wheels
lets his name shimmer in the underground.

A cruel reflective shop window
absorbs noisy street scenes.
The posters of a jazz festival sing
from the façades for some school girls.

A hotel room as a birthday gift.
A voice that is lost in the Po Valley.
The imagination seeks an accomplice.
This city playfully tears a century to pieces.

# BODY LANGUAGE

I draw a chair
and you sit down on it.

I name the sun
and it makes you blink.

I dream a table
and you join me for dinner.

I say the word water
and you rinse your mouth with it.

I invent something about love
and you smile at me.

I point to a bed in which no one has slept
and you suppress a yawn.

I shout up at the sky
and you unfurl your wings.

I snap you with my camera
and time is captured in your eyes.

I sneak up on your sleeping body
and your breathing captivates me.

I read a book and on each page
the letters spell your name.

I tell the day about you loudly
and you vanish silently in the night.

I conceal you in a somber landscape
and you become a river of light.

I look up at the moon
and see it has your face.

# CENSUS AT THE BEGUIN CONVENT

Someone turns off the moonlight.
Someone else lights up the sun.
A third makes the world turn far too quickly.
A fourth goes in search of the stars.
A fifth starts the third world war.
A sixth injures his soul.
A seventh sounds the death toll every hour.
An eighth invents peace.
A ninth composes a national anthem for migrants.
A tenth builds a road which leads to the end of the world.
An eleventh rewrites the Bible.
A twelfth swears like a displaced apostle.
A thirteenth completes the dozen.

# GOD'S DREAM

If it's true that we're
all only characters
inhabiting God's great
endless dream, then he's also
dreaming all our dreams and has no
power to interfere in our existence
since he's not conscious of it.
That he's invented in his dream
Shakespeare as much as Eichmann
testifies to his fantastic imagination.
When the time comes for him
to wake from this nightmare, perhaps he'll
create some divine Freud
who will analyze this dream
and explain it. Then will appear
from what complexes God suffers.
In the future then we shall
likely experience a calmer existence,
but if the therapy miscarries
we're in for stranger
stories yet.

# WITH FRED BERVOETS IN MOSCOW

October in Moscow, with a late after taste
of September, this is what people in this town
call the season of disguised decay,
in which the past love is slowly consumed
but sometimes also preserved, fragile as a relic.

Once he was in the Nevada desert.
Now we stand together on a steep escalator
that pushes us further into the subway
and deep beneath Moscow he closes his eyes
and says: "I've become an old Russian."
Yet he washes ashore every morning
among the pale remains of his friends
who have fed his fantasy in the night.

Even in front of the lawn with the statue
of Mayakovsky Fred Bervoets checks whether the city
is still legible. Life remains unpredictable,
so it is like making a painting.
Sometimes he stops and with broad gestures
he tells about what he saw yesterday
in the streets and cafés of Moscow,
as he tells in his paintings

how life has mistreated him,
how his soul became scarred.

He is looking for his shadow in Red Square.
"I am amazed how beautiful the women
here are, and sometimes how lonely", he says.
"But they have such beautiful eyes."
And he draws the silhouette in space
from Olessia, his Russian guide and interpreter.
Then he falls on his knees before her,
like he does in one of his paintings
and she becomes untouchable, perfect,
with hands folded on chest
as if hidden under a glass dome.

What are his wet fingers saying? That it's raining.
Paint is hidden in his taciturn hair.
Sometimes he would like to shift day into night.
And his beard rips open every time he laughs.

He drinks his beer, which is called pivo here,
alternating with vodka, which resembles water.
"More pivo", he says, probably in the same tone
that Goethe once said "More light."

In the university his big canvases succeed
in confounding the walls of the halls.

The joy of painting
still resonates in the aggressive figures,
piled up and overwhelmed
with a jumble of events.
And look, the line went on the color and
underlines the beauty of the ugly.

No anatomy but expression,
his wild and broad sweeps of red and black
making last night's dream come true
with lines and scratches and curses,
a larynx full of paint slurry,
a net of painted fish,
and he, carefully climbing the stairs,
dead silent, with shoes in hand,
afraid of the harsh blame, the screaming
of the furious, seething woman.

No anatomy but expression,
a stuttering hero in the theater
of the exhibition hall.

# REPETITIONS

## 1

What there is for the first time
always remains irreplaceable.
A repetition is but an imitation
more or less a resemblance.
No single silence is
like the first silence.
In the beginning there was a great void.
With each newly created void
another was always added,
a revised story of the creation.
Repetition does not exist.

## 2

Repetition does not exist.
Each second you are someone else.
Everything is always different.
Time and space change all that exists.
Nothing returns in the form it once was.
Every resemblance rests
on careless observation.
Everything you experience

you experience for the first time.
Everything you experience
you experience for the last time.

**3**

Everything you experience
you experience for the last time.
I am repeating what I already said
and yet I am saying something new.
Barely perceptible changes
occur and deceive the eye.
The word repetition
written twice in a row
does not have the same effect
as the word blue
written twice in a row.

**4**

The word blue
written in blue
is not the same as
the word blue
written in red.
No image is immune.
A dull gray surface with traces

which show the slavery of freedom.
A fullness which runs dry,
a void which is filled,
the endless variation of nothing.

## 5

So many reasons to think
that it could alway be different.
So many attempts are undertaken
with constantly differing results.
If you are already so far down the road
there is no point in turning back
to what has become a memory.
A hand seeks on the paper
the first word that was written,
the first line that was drawn.
Every repetition is a new beginning

## 6

It is just like a landscape
that vanishes quite gradually,
becoming steadily more blurred,
and then becoming visible again,
but, like everything else, is doomed nonetheless
to ultimately disappear.

The longer you look at it
the less recognizable it becomes.
Every detail changes but
seems to return, revised,
as if touched by an alien hand.

# Autumn in New York

As April always will be the perfect month
when blossoming cherry trees color Paris avenues
and hold drops of light between their branches,

so autumn is the season for New York
when nostalgic Charlie Parker dreams
of a hotel room on the 32nd floor

with a mirror that suddenly explodes
then the freed image scampers down the stairs
to disappear into the canyons of glass and steel.

For those who arrive by boat, the town seems like
an ever-enlarging photo.
The surprise comes slowly to its contradiction.
The Statue of Liberty sets fire to a cloud.

A day disappears unknown from the calendar.
The leaves in Central Park always die earlier.
On Fifth Avenue taxis line up in a yellow fever.

Watery skyscrapers absorb the sunlight.
And the Guggenheim Museum counts its circles.
In Washington Square chess players

play the longest match of the year.

Sarah Vaughan sings the metastasis
of nostalgia for this city.
The native remains deaf
to the call of the other towns.

And love? It flames high.
And cries out.

# BILLIE'S BLUES

In every hotel room every time
she meets an older self in the mirror.
Then, as if to banish the light,
Billie Holiday throws up her hand.

On a sleepless Sunday of heroin
the moon drops into her body.
Sadness takes hold of the flower
withering in her hair.

In the nightclub the myth,
has surrounded her for centuries.
She hears the flutter of angels' wings
and every day she becomes fine and mellow.

She puts down the telephone, surprised
that life has already worn itself out.
Her body falls like an avalanche.
Her voice melts away slowly.
Then the world turns to dead silence
and becomes all blue.

# CHARLES BAUDELAIRE IN BRUSSELS

With a burning suitcase full of melancholy
Baudelaire leaves for Brussels April 24th 1864
in order to escape his creditors
and in the hope of finding a publisher
for his collected poems which he sees
exploding at every corner of the street.
He dreams of a black goddess
in a room at the Hôtel du Grand Miroir,
28 rue de la Montagne, whose inner courtyard
is decorated with a golden fountain gushing out time.

The hell of his memory takes him back
to the time of his journey to Calcutta
where he almost dissolved
into the realms of death,
before he had gone past Mauritius.

A spine-chilling instinct haunts him
like dreams under a tropical wind
and gentle reproaches resound from his bed.

The poet wants to flee but hangs on to his image
in the mirror. It is raining on his soul.
A lake forms in the depths of his eyes.
Five fingers drop from each hand.

In a fervent moment he discovers
the artificial paradise of hashish.
He thrusts a dagger at night,
and is blinded by its own light.

He tears himself loose from his body
and becomes a word that floats in the air.

He strolls in imaginary streets,
touches the consciousness of the early morning,
evokes the perfume of dreamt-up women,
distractedly caresses the ebony of his mistress,
meanwhile, the town crackles in his fingers.

Porte de Namur, he walks slowly,
with a dandified, almost feminine, gait
on a slope of the ground.

With his brilliant white collar he appears
at once a clergyman and actor.

On the top of his lacquered leather shoes
he jumps elegantly over the puddles.
He looks at his reflection in all the shop windows
and searches for evil in the accursed words
like flowers blooming on paper.

He draws a diagonal line through suffering,
Invents the beauty of prostitution,
of the wrinkled skins of old women,
who have suffered much from their lovers,
their children or through their own fault.

His body, wracked by syphilis,
bears the patina of strange demons
such as paralysis and problems of speech.
When his memories have paled,
his face is deconstructed in a lighted shop window
and becomes a drawing by Matisse.

The town yelps behind the peeling façades
and reveals another perspective on misery.
How sadly sings decline in the badly-lit room
where the solitary poet lies amidst empty bottles
and thinks of the cruel creole, Jeanne Duval,
she of the gentle black breasts,
the mumbling sources of his sadness.
He strokes the beauty of her scars
and becomes the dearest friend of his shadow.

At the church of Saint-Loup in the city Namur
he sees his friend Félicien Rops blurr
and disappear into the rustling of the night.

He dies in the arms of his mother
who never understood him.

In Montparnasse, one sometimes hears him
still groaning and swearing in his tomb.
And each time a wild flower rises,
it utters the new name of evil.

## IMAGINARY PORTRAIT OF MARC MENDELSON

But who is this strange character?
Nothing more than a head shaped like a bean
(in a fixed position looking left)
but placed on a pedestal.
And always this waving drawing
awkward like an uncertain child
climbing a ladder towards the moon.

A bunch of bananas follows.
Seen strutting about on display
in a Spanish shop window.

Here in Palamos where Marc Mendelson
lives in a quivering white house
with the violent signature
of the sun on its façade.

Allusions to reality,
chain reaction of images
which stop suddenly
petrified in a white dream.

The day of his birth in 1915
London flows slowly into the Thames
who loses its memory on reaching the estuary.

Clouds hook themselves onto the sky
refuse to travel any longer
with the wind and gush out
as depressing downpours.

The season smells like spring.
His mother dances an English waltz
and his father suppresses his feelings
for the cathedral of Antwerp
and for this other powerful river
where grays grimace and wharfs abound.

The Spanish walls are covered with signs
living synthesis of a life,
flagrant worship of matter.
The world is hiccuping and spinning shockingly.

Late in September, like a cry in the morning
appears at last anew the prospect
neglected for years in the brouhaha
of fantastic inscriptions wearing away.

In an aquarelle he reveals
a Spanish sky of such a clear blue
with underneath a sea bluer still
and at the border of the two halves
which sway oppressively in thick black lines,
the outline of a little boat;
again like a child would make.

Manuscript of a magician.
The pictorial language is captive
in a prison of paper
hesitant meander of ideas
on a monochrome surface.

In the street the sun thunders down.
A shadow crosses the wall.
All the branches bear green words.

But in the seams of language
a forgotten word gets stuck.
And he? What else is he other
than the name of a body.
A gust of wind lifts it all away.

# The Swimmer in the Sky

## 1

Grown old and faded the clouds tear
sliding slowly across the eternal blue.
Yet the sun quivers heedlessly.
Someone is recklessly stepping out of the landscape.

Then the swimmer appeared in the sky.
He goes up and down on waves of sound.
Heavenly music surrounds him on all sides
but like a river rising he evades the dance.

Over the roofs he gives a light cry
and with despairing gestures dives away
behind a cloud white with powerless rage.
Someone passes, shrugs his shoulders.

## 2

With slow strokes he digs
deep waves in the clouds.
His hair hangs tangled
over his wetly shining brow.

Seen from above
everything seems much more real.
The people and objects down there
are all made of dust.

His body glistens in the sun.
Is he copper or bronze?
Calmly he swims on towards his goal,
an invisible but tangible existence.

## 3

He is an archeologist of the heavens.
Sometimes he dives and picks up the rest.
Resting on the bed of space.
Weightless objects like ghosts and gods.

Things astronauts have forgotten
float whirling by.
Silence and emptiness wait somewhere
where a black hole has been painted.

## 4

So many anxieties he has already survived.
At night he swims among the stars.
Patiently he tidies up the mess

left behind by the Little Bear.
Then the sun rises again.
Shyly he looks at the gleam of morning.
Suddenly Icarus whirrs past him.
A white head of foam blooms up
all around the hard and merciless splash.
A dream vanished forever in the sea.

## 5

He swims through a crack in the light
and arrives among all sorts
darting and merrily dancing, drunk
in the joy of never having existed.
Harried and hurried by the shadows
of his unbelief he recognises,
wallowing wearily, bemused and amazed
in the hot violence of the firmament,
the hiccup of the Earth slamming shut.

## 6

Dripping with his blindingly white light
in which all lies are the preys of prayers,
he is accosted by silence and homesickness.
In the clouds he rewrites his life.
Beneath him it is snowing while he sings

the high song of the archangel who has,
like a young bank clerk, embezzling the sun.

## 7

The swimmer now causes a stir in the sky.
The papers write lyrically about him.
The TV newscast will not let him go.
After his seventh orbit of the Earth
he grows a little tired of all the fuss.
He is even almost canonized.
In Rome someone even spoke of a miracle.
Then the swimmer took a resolute decision
and vanished unnoticed into someone's dream.

# OBVIOUS BEAUTY

Just as everything becomes breathtaking
where she is concerned,
so will be my love for her.

Just as the weightless drowned man
floating up and down very slowly
his mouth open in amazement,
inhales the softness of the water.

Just as the invisible hunter
strides proudly through the forests
and makes the dark trees
disappear one by one into his game bag.

Like the cry of a night bird
tears the white of the sheet,
she turns and turns in her sleep
and every time she gets more beautiful.

# African Queen

Nothing of her will pass away.
The mirror holds on to her image.
The bed keeps the exact shape
of her body stretched there.
The fullness of her mouth,
the smoothness of her knees,
nothing will ever be lost.
Her odor itself has grown
into me. And all that she said
is present, she can never vanish,
even though invisible now.
Her tongue put love through its paces.
Her hands made tenderness a story.
Everything she caressed of me is gone,
is now with her, is now hers.
I know still how things were
when she was present. I am looking at her
even if she is no longer there.

# THE HOUSE

In front of the house a fleck of sunlight waits
for the moment to pounce on a shadow.
The linden tree whispers its secrets
behind a mask of dry leaves.

In the living room the table
collects her brood of chairs around her.
The chairs laugh amongst themselves
at the longing of the table.

In a dark corner the sideboard growls,
behind the glass doors the glasses stand
full of tears.

Decay falls out of the hearth.
A lamp looks for colors
on the wall. A stain falters.

Warmth spreads
like a dark body
sinking in the sea of silence.

Outside the street falls asleep.
The sun becomes a blind eye.

# THE INVENTION OF TENDERNESS

Everything falls silent at this moment.
No object still dares to breathe.
Silence comes to rest in this emptiness.

Among the softest creases of the bed
you very gradually became visible,
with your darkest smile full of melancholy,
for what shall know no repetition.

The words you said were charged
with the languidness of longing.

And after you had gone
I noticed that you have taken
all the colors of the landscape with you.
What remained was nothing but gray.

It was then that someone
invented tenderness. A discovery
that almost moved him to tears.

# A CASE OF AMNESIA

It was only after billions of years
that God having become old and long in the tooth
no longer followed the course of things so carefully
and could no longer manage everything.
The stars and the planets that he used
to put in place according to a scrupulously-established plan,
still submissively followed their pre-established path.
But now and again one
would escape and, attracted by another star,
would collide noisily with it.

It happened also that God forgot something
because little black holes formed
in his enormous memory full of his omnipotence.
Gradually forgetfulness set in.
First of all he forgot that humans are sometimes unhappy
following arguments or accidents more or less serious.
In spite of their cries, he didn't hear
because he was starting to become hard of hearing.

Then he forgot that men were imprisoned for years
because they had demanded justice from the authorities.
He forgot the thieves, the rapists and the murderers.

He even forgot that wars had broken out
and he let the fires rage madly
without intervening to relieve the suffering.

Finally he forgot that he had created the world
and that man was threatening to destroy this world.

When he noticed one day, to his great astonishment,
that all his creation had been ruined forever,
he decided to go back to his original plan.
He vacuumed the cosmos until there was a complete void.
All the stars disappeared from the firmament.
Worn out, God, who at the time
was also suffering from Parkinson's disease,
lay on his back to die in peace.
He contentedly looked at the infinite void
where calm and silence had returned.

Except that he had forgotten one little thing, a tiny astronaut
who was floating alone in space like an insect.
When God, completely exhausted, expired,
there remained in space the brilliant laugh
of the astronaut, who, everything considered, was right.
But there was no one any more
who had read his books
or knew his name: Friedrich Nietzsche.

# THE USEFULNESS OF POETRY

There are few things in the world as useless as a poem.
Because everything important in this life
has no commercial value.
There is nothing that can be done with a poem.
A broker doesn't know how to recommend it.
A lawyer doesn't know what to do with it.
A politician can't exploit it.
A thief won't steal it.
A soldier will not want to destroy it.

Each poem is a sort of lunar eclipse
but it can also be something completely different:
a verse never to be forgotten,
an image which obsesses you,
a combination of words which continues to intrigue you.

Some, like Jan Slauerhoff, can live in their poems.
Others, like Maurice Gilliams, stuff them into a bottle,
which they throw purposely into the sea.
Again others, like J. Bernlef, blow them up.
As for the rest, one can't get anywhere
with a poem, except for the strange and poetic sensation
that something good and defenseless

can last longer
than suppression of individual expression,
piling up of enemy bodies,
burning of a conquered town.

# Vision Under Water

He stands upright with leaden shoes
planted firmly on the bottom of the sea.

His lustrous hair sways back and forth
trailing the currents of the water.

His eyes and mouth are open wide,
the fish say hello as they pass.

He seems at times to grope with one hand
at something dancing around him.

He appears to take a curious pleasure
in all that happens here below.

And each time the sun touches the horizon
you can hear him shout the inaudible.

# MAURICE WYCKAERT AIRBORNE

He paints the top of the clouds
and puts together parcels of fields
which he drops into the deepness along a crack
at the precise point where they belong.

He describes how a far way from beneath him,
at the place where the earth breathes and seduces,
the countryside twists itself like flames,
without the least desire for a horizon.

The wind chases the birds out of the sky.
Because here is the painter's domain.
All that lives is forever banished
or covered with a thick layer of paint.

The first landscape still joyfull danced
through the mists of William Turner.
Later, Wyckaert with Asger Jorn, discovers
the body of Italy bathing in the past.

And insatiable light touches
his hands when they scratch into the anterior,
the knife scrapes and draws
signs which again soak up the light.

Like Hölderlin, he reads the clouds,
which are unreachable, and always escape.
Under them, the fields were stretched out,
by a gentle hand, undivided, ambiguous.

And the light remains insatiable
while the fields unfold their primary colors
and creak at each change of season.
The landscape takes on the flavor of aniseed.

A new painting is falling out of the clouds.
A struggle with uncertainty remains,
quickly layered onto the canvas, squeezed from the tube
just like life existing in profusion.

Each season hesitates and stumbles.
Winter slides in oily paint.
Springtime: waiting for cruel antlers
which grow before your eyes like bars.
He paints standing up, detecting
the essence of life,
with large gestures and generous surfaces of colour.
In this way, he unveils the transcendence.

The clouds stray in phonemes
so much so that the perspective chokes
in his rendering of the phenomena

such as warm and cold, red or blue.

Red is life which simmers.
As to the painter, he grows lonely
under the luminous sign of nature
that stays awake, changing from hour to hour.

In the morning the colours squabble
and the awakening countryside creaks
even in its smallest cracks of happiness.
The past has many dwelling places.

In the heat of July he suddenly died.
Precious liberty then dissolves into space.
All that he dreamed of survives in painting.
Each landscape remembers his hand.

# A MOTHER'S LOVE

Often memory works like a photograph.
An old image suddenly returns,
where nothing moves
as if time decided to have a break.
The mother is still sitting in the same chair.

You can bring her face closer.
you then observe on her eyes
a thin liquid veil which vibrates,
not quite real tears, and yet,
like the very beginning of sorrow.

Placed in her lap, her hands
a light brown, like fallen leaves,
sink into a cloud of nostalgia.
And I, still a child, I rest my head,
my cheek with a red scar,
on the hard curves of her knees.
Years later she lets me go
and I learn the solitude of adults.

# AMERICAN SILENCE

*Silence is so accurate*
Mark Rothko

When someone finally understood
the (real) meaning of the words
most of the angels rose and slowly
danced the silent rounds of the last morning.

At that moment Mark Rothko invented red.
He turned the silence into a rectangle.
Then the hush began in all colors.

Someone then took advantage of the time
to hide all his bewilderment in it.
Nothing more, nothing reached our ears anymore.
Resonances were never heard again.

He playfully spelled the salty alphabet of the sea.
Secretly he committed the first act
after which his hands became unreachable.

Tenderly, he read the words one by one.
He began involuntarily with the word I.
He used the dead voice of a long-forgotten poet.

# SOCRATES DRINKS

I cannot think of an acceptable reason
why should I refuse this decorated cup?
Besides, this drink tastes like an incantation
and it was a wise decision, taken by
the wise men of this city, gracious in their betrayal.

Maybe I was indeed the menacing weed.
In a white robe, I became hoarse and black.
The fathers read constellations and see their sons
playing with arguments and thoughts. They regret
this as a battered time in which doubt grew.

I know I will slip away singing very softly
in an endless sleep that will eventually teach me
something, the childish word that no one knows.
Their imagination falls short. Never will they
see my shadow in this imaginary garden.

# ENVOI

I write so my death will sound senseless.
I'm silent to hear you speak quietly in me,
to hear you say that from now on and
every day I will bear yet another name, that I
will walk again in the guise of another body.
For I create reality anew each time
and want to eat with my mouth full from this moment
in which I am named everywhere and deafeningly grow
into this mysterious key that fits the night
when everything glows that never happened
except in words.

Because I carry truth in me like a heart,
I am pressed to speak a word as big as myself,
I, who rarely exist any larger than life-size,
to shiver on liquid feet
on the cold ground of being,
where freezing rain leaves a thin crust of sadness,
covering the past without a sound.
Simplicity always speaks for itself.
Melancholy is always about you and then
and sometimes a bit about me.

# Biographical Information

**Willem Maurits Roggeman** is a Belgian poet, novelist, and art critic. His poetry has been widely translated, and he is a regular guest at international poetry festivals. He has also published two novels and several collections of articles on artists and highly

regarded interviews with writers. In 1988, he was awarded the Order of Leopold II for his cultural work. His most recent book of poems is *Bewegend portret* (2022).

**Philippe Ernewein** is a native of Turnhout, Belgium. He is the Director of Education at the Denver Academy in Denver, Colorado, USA. Philippe's published work can be found at www.rememberit.org.

Willem M. Roggeman & Philippe Ernewein, November 2019, Brussels, Belgium

112 N. Harvard Ave. #65
Claremont, CA 91711

chapbooks@bamboodartpress.com
www.bamboodartpress.com

CPSIA information can be obtained
at www.ICGtesting.com
Printed in the USA
BVHW080123130123
656250BV00023B/223

9 781947 240650